Presented to

BENJAMIN STADULIS

Welcome To Religious School

October 15, 1995
22 Tishrei 5756

by

Har Sinai Hebrew Congregation
Trenton, New Jersey

Rabbi David E. Straus
Cantor David S. Wisnia
Ann W. Kanarek, Director

GATES
of
WONDER

Texts by

Robert Orkand
Joyce Orkand
Howard I. Bogot

Illustrated and Designed by

Neil Waldman

Chair, Committee on Children's Liturgy
Kenneth D. Roseman

I.S.B.N. No. 0-88123-009-X

GATES of WONDER

A Prayerbook for Very Young Children

The publication of this prayerbook is made possible
by the generosity of members of the Westchester Reform
Temple in honor of their beloved rabbi,
Rabbi Jack Stern

CENTRAL CONFERENCE OF AMERICAN RABBIS

We need time to pray.

Prayer is talking to God.

Prayer is talking about God.

When we pray we think

about our lives.

Prayers help us.

בָּרוּךְ אַתָּה יְיָ!

Ba-ruch A-ta A-do-nai!

It is important for us

to pray to God.

7

When I pray I wonder...

I wonder what *Mitzvah* is;

I wonder about rainbows.

I wonder about day and night.

11

I wonder if I could touch

the stars.

I wonder what I'll be like

when I'm older.

I wonder why people are different.

I wonder when all people will be safe.

I wonder about life.

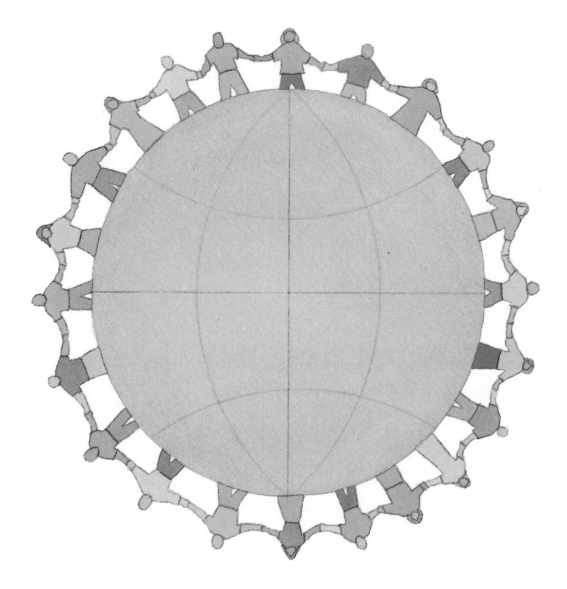

17

Wondering is

reaching for answers.

בָּרְכוּ אֶת יְיָ הַמְבֹרָךְ!

Ba-re-chu et A-do-nai

ha-me-vo-rach!

בָּרוּךְ יְיָ הַמְבֹרָךְ לְעוֹלָם וָעֶד!

Ba-ruch A-do-nai ha-me-vo-rach

le-o-lam va-ed!

God is forever!

Prayer is reaching for God.

19

One person can
make a difference.
One me, one you,
caring for each other.

We pray for a world

with people living in peace.

One Mitzvah helps me
do more Mitzvot.

One Shabbat each week.

One Torah to study.

One God!

שְׁמַע יִשְׂרָאֵל יְיָ אֱלֹהֵינוּ, יְיָ אֶחָד!

She-ma Yis-ra-eil Adonai E-lo-hei-nu,

Adonai E-chad!

God is One!

בָּרוּךְ שֵׁם כְּבוֹד מַלְכוּתוֹ לְעוֹלָם וָעֶד!

Ba-ruch sheim ke-vod mal-chu-to

le-o-lam va-ed!

God is always part of the world!

25

We learn about God in Torah.

וְאָהַבְתָּ אֵת יְיָ אֱלֹהֶיךָ.

Ve-a-hav-ta eit Adonai E-lo-hei-cha.

We can teach others about God.

We think about God

when we get up.

We think about God

when we go to school.

We think about God

when we play.

29

We think about God

when we go to bed.

We think about God

all the time.

מִי שֶׁ

God acts in special ways.

We can be special, too.

35

We can sing about God.

מִי כָמֹכָה בָּאֵלִם, יְיָ? מִי כָּמֹכָה

נֶאְדָּר בַּקֹּדֶשׁ, נוֹרָא תְהִלֹת עֹשֵׂה פֶלֶא?

Mi cha-mo-cha ba-ei-lim, Adonai?

Mi ka-mo-cha, ne-dar ba-ko-desh,

no-ra te-hi-lot, o-sei fe-leh?

Who can be like God?

I can!

God acts in special ways.

I can be special, too.

Tov le-ho-dot la-a-do-nai...
Saying thank you to God
is good.

Praying to God is special.

God is wonderful!

God is One!

שְׁמַע יִשְׂרָאֵל: יְיָ אֱלֹהֵינוּ, יְיָ אֶחָד!

בָּרוּךְ אַתָּה, יְיָ אֱלֹהֵינוּ, מֶלֶךְ הָעוֹלָם, שֶׁהֶחֱיָנוּ וְקִיְּמָנוּ וְהִגִּיעָנוּ לַזְּמַן הַזֶּה.

Ba-ruch a-ta, A-do-nai E-lo-hei-nu, me-lech ha-o-lam, she-he-che-ya-nu ve-ki-ye-ma-nu ve-hi-gi-a-nu la-ze-man ha-zeh.

Thank you, God, for life!

Thank you, God, for caring!

Thank you, God, for this day.

Amen.